NEW ANSWERS FOR OLD AND NEW TESTAMENTS OF GOD IN MY OWN WORDS

My own ways of describe heaven and hell

Kristie Duc

NEW ANSWERS FOR OLD AND NEW TESTAMENTS OF GOD IN MY OWN WORDS MY OWN WAYS OF DESCRIBE HEAVEN AND HELL

iUniverse books may be ordered through booksellers or by contacting:

iUniverse
1663 Liberty Drive
Bloomington, IN 47403
www.iuniverse.com
844-349-9409

Because of the dynamic nature of the Internet, any web addresses or links contained in this book may have changed since publication and may no longer be valid. The views expressed in this work are solely those of the author and do not necessarily reflect the views of the publisher, and the publisher hereby disclaims any responsibility for them.

Any people depicted in stock imagery provided by Getty Images are models, and such images are being used for illustrative purposes only. Certain stock imagery © Getty Images.

ISBN: 978-1-6632-4274-7 (sc)
ISBN: 978-1-6632-4276-1 (hc)
ISBN: 978-1-6632-4275-4 (e)

Library of Congress Control Number: 2022913472

Print information available on the last page.

iUniverse rev. date: 08/10/2022

I n the name of the Father, the Son and the Holly Spirit. We all have to admit we are all God servant. Satan doesn't. No one is more special than God and every one has sin except Mary, the queen of heaven and mother of God. When God choses he is never wrong. Mary is the best person to be a mother of God. We are what we compatible to our personality or our choices of race before we were born. If you are one race and look like some other race because you have mixed up personality. God didn't appoint us to be that race, he didn't make our souls either. If you are black and have black personality, and can deal with black people and be close to them better, you wouldn't want to be inside an Asian or white body or vise versa, so don't ask why God didn't make us all the same, because black people wouldn't often want to marry Asians or other race or some Asian don't want to marry other Asian or every other races. Some Asian have mix personalities like me so I look like part Asian, part white, and part black, or part of some other races even I'm pure, not mixed. Some love black spouse, some love white, some love to hang out with pretty sexy girls, and some only like to marry ugly girl whom give them control or vice versa or both. Some wants a lot of children, some just like to have a lover. We are all different so there is no limit of discussing problems about choices about people. So don't discuss. Just enjoy life. God knew we are sinners but have somewhat good in us so he makes a body and give to us so we can be existed. God is a human before us. He needs to be born visibly, even he didn't have to be born on earth instead of born in heaven. He has all kind of weakness, but he won them all. God rule the world we just have to follow his teaching but we didn't. But God knows his children is enjoying lives and forgot so he just wanted to remind us he is still there to take care of us, punishing to make better, clean our souls so we will not be out of control and will be tempted by Satan to be in eternal hell. Our lives pass by very fast. Eternity is billion times more important. Thank God for the life he gave to us if there is hardship that is good for the souls. The more God cleans our souls the faster way to get to heaven. Log, the man whom were punished by God in every way but still give thanks. That kind of people God loves most. Satan is not a goat image like with two short or long horns. He looks scarier than any statue we made of him. Some Satan worshippers think Satan is a very handsome man. He was. But not anymore. Satan will look like what he do harm to us. Satan will look like all accidents we had, how disaster our corps are that's what

NEW ANSWERS FOR OLD AND NEW TESTAMENTS
OF GOD IN MY OWN WORDS

he will look like, multiplied million times if he harmed millions. He has to endure constantly his changing images of disaster corps which were what he tempted we do to each other. Satan even made us blame God and hate God for what we've done to each other. And we will become Blasphemer, This sin will automatically make us belong to Satan and we will not be protect by God, we will eventually be in eternal hell after death. If ever we feel like hating God, we must constantly ask God to forgive because we are being possessed by the devil. The Antichrist, and all devil worshippers of must pray for God protection before it's too late. Satan is very strong because of these people. They have misconceptions about Satan, and

5

forgot that God made this world, our bodies and everything came from God. But Satan claimed he can give all to us. The virgin Mary, mother of God once taught us to pray: Dear father, forgive our sins, bring all souls to heaven, especially those whom needed most. She was indicating the Satan worshippers, because she visited hell often and could not get them out of there. Purgatory is like jails on earth. We still have hope, even some place in purgatory looks like hell. Some small crimes or very serious crimes we did on earth has to pay all our sins on earth or in purgatory after death before we can go to heaven. Jesus did not appear often but he let his mother appeared more than 300 times on earth because he doesn't want us to think he is in favor of these places and not other. Those places is message for disasters or hardships will occur some where on earth The end of the world will happen when these Satan worshippers won't change and dedicated their souls to devils forever, that is when Jesus come down and claim his people. We will be eternally in Heaven with God, no more miseries or sorrows nor death nor sickness. We will still meet our families just like now, and they still can be far away in other places and visit us. If we happened to have a Satan disguised as our family member and do all kind of serious crimes and hated God, God will erase them from our memories so we won't feel sad after we go to heaven and they go to hell. Heaven might be here too, like

Garden of Eden was on earth. But we don't have to work unless we want to, everything will be easier, If we wanted to hunt for sports God will make fake animals look exactly the same and can move or eat or breath but they won't feel the pain when got shot at. All animals will be nice and adorable like when they were in the Garden of Eden. We all love to have bear, lion, tiger, monkey, all kinds of animal we adore by choices will be in our back yards, they will be very meek. Sins of the world made them very harmful and brought death to us in every way, but at the end of the world, which will be the most scary three days of darkness, Satan will claim his people and Jesus will claim his and will bring all of us to heaven, no more death.

Pets and animals react very fast so we thought they have more senses and more emotions than us, but that is only their intuitions, they react like a machine. So don't worry too much, they won't feel sad or depress or worry, even their reactions look like that. They don't think and don't keep in their souls because they have no souls. Even when they memorized thins it's just like a memorized machine, no grudge or emotions, even they can see love and react to love, but they can't feel love. They can protect their cubs by seeing love, but they can forget their cubs forever when they grew up and lived apart, they won't remember., unless their cubs grew up and live within their territories they might recognize and protect each other. Animal or pets have duties to protect and feed and pamper their cubs and have relationships. But they don't have goals for eternal lives after death nor future plans. They just do everything by intuitions, like a machine need a plug to work, or some parts need other parts, and Because human have souls and mind so they have to think first before react, but animals don't, so they react right away, but it's not that they are more obey or more emotional or more love but it's the opposite. They don't get depress or worry extensively, but they do have the senses to react to survive. But they don't have mercy for other animals, nor malice nor grudge, but they will kill whenever or whatever the reason is. We all tend to be very sad and depress when

our adorable pet died. But we don't know that
animal don't want to live that long, so God
limited their years to minimum of 15 years or
so. Imagine if they have to listen to us when or
what they want to eat, sleep or hike not on their
time but ours. And they couldn't talk, couldn't
buy stuff, couldn't drive nor ride nor take bath
by themselves. A live like that is not a happy
live. But they still don't recognize that problem.
They look very happy more than our children
when we got home. But they are not, they don't
think but just react. But they do have memories
like a machine so they obey in a machinery
way, but not emotional. And so when we gave
them to another owner, they first seems to be
very scare by survival intuitions, but after a few

hours or so they know we are nice, they will be at peace, and no more agitations. God have mercy only give their lives about a decade or more, because God didn't make their intuitions, but because they have intuitions so God made a body for them. Some people saw dog ghost or cat, it's only Satan in disguise, because souls are ghosts, but animal don't have souls. God is the most loving souls he loves animals more than us. If animal can feel depress, happy or grateful than us God already made them human not pets, they might look very depress or sad, but if another stranger or owner come and play with them, they will be very happy and forget About everything, not like us prolong even for many years, or even die of depressions.so enjoy your pets but don't forget our love ones.

Everything is possible. Some people said they came from their pass lives, reincarnation, they didn't lie. Their lives were cut short but it was not time for them to go yet, so God let them have another chance. Hell can be on earth too, if we have no feeling, no mercy and very cruel for no reason or kill people for our thrill, we can die and reincarnations to be an allegator or some other and got kill and eaten by us before they can become human again. Heaven is not a boring place. All saints and God are still working every day to punish, clean and save souls. It's an active place. Adam and Eve, our ancestors didn't have to go through painful labor, God can still give them their own kids through miracle. But because they have sin just like all of us except the Virgin Mary, so we all have to go through life with all the difficulties. Be patient, one hundred years or less passes by very quick. The ancients king or queen did not have the knowledge of the bible so they kept all their processions include their servants to be buried alive with them to be in the other side when they died so they will have some servant after death. Some scientists are very amazed at God's work so they researched and found out why the river at Moses time divided and think it was not a miracle. Could be. But God is the beginning and the end, he put Moses and Pharaoh to be born at the same time when the event of the rising river split into half, and the same time as all the 7 plaques. So those miracles are about when it happened, not why. Some scientist said the river that Moses divide was a very shallow one. That's right. But the unstable violent water could drown all Pharaoh soldiers Scientist believe in God, but their job is to explore. That's how we can learn from them. Some scientist said he went every where in space but couldn't find God. But God is there but he just couldn't see. God did appear as Jesus so many times on earth as the son of Mary and a lot of us don't believe or don't know. So why should he appear again. This world was made out of goodness. Goodness made things possible. God doesn't know why he exist, it's just that he was so good and so perfect no sin at all, so he existed first before anybody or anything. But he is love and love create a God. God doesn't need us, he can manifest good angels out of his souls. God does not responsible for our existences, he is human like us, very busy loving himself like us but he knows that even we will be sinners, not deserve to be born, but he wanted us to be like him to enjoy life, so he made his own body and he made us out of his image. If we don't believe in God, when we die we won't have eternity in heaven with him, but we will be nothing. Mary, mother of God, has to endure her only son being tortured in everyway emotionally, physically, financially and because God is much more sensitive than us, he suffered much more than us. God and his son are one. Jesus inherited his father's name King Of The World and Heaven. God can appear or disappear because in the beginning he is invisible, but he created himself a body, whom is Jesus. We are just souls, but he made us out of his image. So if we don't believe in God or deny him, he will not create a new body for us after we are dead and become dust. And if we are sinners and not believe in God, we will have to pay all our sins before we become nothing. And if we keep fighting with God like Satan and tempt other people to fight God and never quit, our souls will be in hell eternally. God is a soul just like us, goodness made his soul. God didn't make our souls, but we have some good in us so he helped us to have a body to exist. But because only sinless is allow to exist, but God is so good and merciful, even he knew we will do sin by our thoughts, hearts and souls, and even God knew he will have to sacrifice and die for us but he still made us. Not only Adam and Eve but all human race will have sins so we had all kind of hardships emotionally, physically or financially. But in the beginning in the Garden of Eden we human had no worry until we made sin, we were suppose to be extinct, because only goodness is allow to exist from the beginning, but God chose to sacrifice to resume our existences. He made himself a son out of his souls, the son then appear into Mary's womb, the only person in the world is sinless like him.

He made us out of dust and we will be dust at the end. But he will give us a new body. He is human before us. He has all the weakness and all senses like us, but he sacrificed all and gain it all. He was just doing us a favor, by remind us that he already took our place in hell by being crucified, and if we don't accept this grace, we will automatically be nothing like from the beginning when we didn't have a body yet. Angels of different races used to live in the Garden of Eden, which is the earth today, they built, pyramids, giant stones that piles on top of each other when there were no equipment nor machines back then at the early ages. and other statues that moved from many miles away. When we human existed, we just continue their work. Heaven can be seen or unseen, not like earth. Jesus which is God once said to the criminal on the cross: Today you will be with me in paradise." Jesus stayed on earth 40 days after his death, So Jesus is heaven, any where he goes is heaven. He can make heaven disappear or change just like here on earth, we have new design or keep old ones is up to us. Heaven is not a boring place, it just like here but it's better. Hell is getting more spaces because of our sins that built it. Satan is getting more brutal because of our sins, natural disasters is getting worst because of our sins. We created miseries, not God. But whomever died in vain and not deserve to be dead will go to heaven very early, because they've cleaned all their sins.

We all have sins because we are all weak. We are like our kids to God, even we are old we are still just children to God so we need to dedicate our lives to follow the experience one whom has no sin and he is our first father before our earthly father. And because he made our parents, they have to depend on God to raise us. If our parents don't believe in God Satan will take over and ruin our lives. We don't want none of our families to go to hell while we are in heaven. But if the devil disguised as our parents or our child, he or she will be a very bad person, for example, a serial killer and won't repent when we go to heaven God will make us forget about them so we will not feel sad. The problem with Satan is he won't repent and accept God is God so he cannot be saved. We need to love God and not question him. If some religions are not worshipping Jesus, they either never had an opportunity to learn about Jesus whom is the only God, but they still do good deeds, they will go to heaven too. But if some Christians already knew Jesus is an only God and denied or rebel, like the name of Satan means the adversary, they will follow Satan to eternal fire in hell, if they don't repent fast enough before the end of the world. But Satan will not quit tempting them. So never worship Satan from the beginning. That is why we need to ask God every day to protect us even just for a few minutes, tell God we love him and thank him for he died for our existences to continue if not now then eternity in heaven. Some said

God is too strict. No, God is the most generous

in lavishing our needs, but he did spoil Satan

so he from that day get very serious about our

sins because small sins will make bigger sins

and so on and on. Unless we need God to

remind us to cling to him like a boat, because

Satan will constantly tempts us, and worst,

Satan and all his followers like to tempt the

most loving people of God, and if we are not

asking for God's protection every day, we will

eventually denied God and follow Satan. If we

don't have time as we think, just make a sign

of a cross when we wake up or when we go to

sleep and tell Jesus we love him, eventually we

will love God and will love to visit him at

church. But if we don't feel like go to church because everybody is there, we can go alone where there is no mass at any time churches are open. Jesus will be very sad if we don't come to visit him just one hour a week, that is the most important thing in life. But to love God in your heart And think of him, talk to him every day is the most important to. But eventually we will spare one hour every week to visit him at mass and after he changed or lives and we will continue to receive God's grace one way or another, let God decide our graces, don't expect him to do whatever we ask, but to do whatever he will manage with what we ask in order to give us what is right for us. If we make God do what is right for you but not God's plan, we will be like Satan and ruin our lives. People at church have all kind of problem too, we all human are sinners don't feel bad about your sins. A lot of people have worst sins more than us but they are not shy to confess through priests or ministers to the almighty father whom love us so much. Confess them all to the priest and God will listen. Priests or pastors will tell you what to do with your sins. If you are not Christian but you want to be, God will love you very much. You can start praying by yourselves first, and God will give you courage to confess. Miracle happen right away after you feel the love of God, you will feel very peaceful and will believe in God whom is Jesus. There was no evil on earth until our sins created a monster, and that monster appear to tempt Adam and Eve, Cain and so on and on. And all the sins and rebellious of us people create a more sinister monster named Satan, he was a prince and a belove creation of God, but our sins made him more brutal. So God had to be born through his son body to pay for our sins. The greatest grace is to be born again without sin and belong to Jesus. if we are too busy just keep a picture of Jesus, tell him you love him. If not we will eventually not do anything right without him protecting us. Love is first most prefer by Jesus, equal to the rules of church, but if you are not ready to go to church school, eventually you will love church, now you don't and don't worry too much if you are not

Christians, or you are a lost Christian and went through all miseries in lives. Do not be discourage, all the people whom success in life they either miserable when they were young or even they will be miserable in the future, nobody is certain for the future, so don't be discourage and never commit suicide. God made everybody equal, success people worked very hard, they either have problems not about financially, but other problem we didn't know so don't compare. Some poor people are more happy than some rich people, and vice versa. Just be happy and thank God. Just tell our father every day we need him, always put his picture near you so it will remind us to say hi to Jesus, don't forgot to kiss his feet. If you have a picture of the crucifixion of Christ, kiss on his palm, head or feet where he hurt. God is still hurt because of our sins. Jesus is human, he like us to be close to him every day, respectfully and proudly because we have a father as an almighty God, with all the miracles he did when he lived with us thousands of years ago. not just a statue or an unknown invisible God far away like some people are still worshiping, even they are not sure what he is like, how nice or cruel he is, a God like that whom never appear nor sacrificed, is too scary. We have families, pictures, histories and everything visible to be mingle with our friends and our love ones, God deserve that more than us. He doesn't need us like we need him. Tears

go down not up, just like when we become
parents, we will know the feelings of God's
love. God once said anybody loves their families
more than him is not worth his. God doesn't
want or have time to interfere with our lives,
he is just doing us a favor. Without God, Satan
will tempt families to hate and kill each other.
Love God with all your heart, mind and soul
even in miseries, we will surely have a free
ticket to go to heaven, where all the things we
need is there, or all the love we want. We can
only have love through God. His nick name is
love. Jesus did not made out of sperm nor eggs,
but he was made out of love, so he will give love
to us through other people, our folks and
friends and strangers. we will not have wars in

heaven and we will all live peacefully. We can travel by air plane or fly with our own wings. We can work if we are addicted to work, or we can retire and go gamble, clubs, sports. We will never have any problem because our guardian angels will be beside us to guide. Angels are spirits that only like to be souls. Angels like to be just living lightly, like priest on earth some are very dedicate to their job and live with the love of the Lord. Heaven is just like here on earth. We can still get marry or we can live like angels worry free. We can meet our family on earth they will be there too. Or you can create a new family, like Log, he was taken away all people in his family but he gain new one. Maybe he owns their love from the past so he had to pay back for a while and then they became strangers, and he had to marry again to make another family. Everything is possible. Just like here on earth, when God made human and earth, he didn't want to be different from heaven. If not, we are just a whole bunch of strangers to him like aliens. Aliens might be some dead people or abortions souls come to earth to get revenge, and is very hard for us to fight, because they can disappear. With the love of God we will do everything good for our souls. Give your love to him you can receive anything you deserve. No need to worry even today you are the most miserable, tomorrow will be another day. Jesus said let tomorrow take care of tomorrow, without God if you are a billionaire you still feel miserable. Must give Jesus a few minutes a day and give him love and ask for protections. If not all the devil are waiting to take your grace away by make you leaving Jesus, eventually you will suffer and only wait for Satan mercy, but he will deceive you to be very powerful in a sinful way, until you died and go to hell with him, and there is nothing in hell like Satan promise. When we are still alive even if we lost everything, we still can gain everything we want with God, not in death.so repent and cling to Jesus as soon as possible. It will not be right away what you ask for, but it's a test. Like Log lost everything but he still loved and praised God. That kind of people God love the most. remember only God

NEW ANSWERS FOR OLD AND NEW TESTAMENTS
OF GOD IN MY OWN WORDS

can fight Satan. Without him even if we are good, we will become bad. So go with our creator. Abortions are not our privilege. Embryos are God s creation just like he created us. If we kill them, our hope, our lives will be taken away or will be miserable like them, because they lost all the hope. Jesus was made out of love not sperm nor egg. But he has to go through all stage in the embryo to mingle with us so we can be close to him. But God was a most gentle sweet and kind Jesus, What a blessing for humanity. Abraham was our faith ancestor. He was as good as Mary. But God deserve to have a loving mother and she is the best one on earth. She went through all the sacrifices just like Jesus. God's family is the most loving family. We can share their love and we will be at peace, if not in this life, then eternity. Sacrifice and follow Jesus. he will wipe our tears just like he wiped his own and his family tears. Now they are in heaven. In heaven is the most enjoyable place. God made the earth only six days, heaven must be spectacular. I once had a dream of heaven it looked just like here on earth, but it looked much better don't know why. I even saw Jesus, he looked just like in his picture. Jesus is not Mary's real son so they look different, but the love made them bond more than real mother and son. We are all stranger join together and made a family, God is love he did not come from sperm nor egg, but love is family, not sperm or egg that can become dust when we died but the love is

forever. Sometimes Jesus ask even he knew

everything. Just like parent ask kid do you want

to drink even they knew the kid is thirsty, they

will not just pour water into their kid's mouth.

Jesus said don't cry for him but cry for our

children while carrying his cross. Jesus always

tried to save us. Satan gave hell on earth not

God. Jesus once said some people whom are

not Christians and don't know Jesus will go to

heaven before bad Christians. And some

already knew Jesus as God and denied him,

they will not be saved after death. Please return

to God. Hell don't have fire but it has invisible

heat that can burn souls. Souls hurts more than

body because senses came from souls,

emotionally and physically. Without soul senses will die. Soul is the electric of body. God blew his soul into our nose so we can feel senses, if not we are just made out of dust. God's souls is our senses, if we don't love him our soul will be contaminate by devil soul, and God will leave us. God is only a soul until he created his own body whom is Jesus. Jesus didn't disobey his mother, but he wanted to let his mother have more faith by being away for 3 days. And after that Mary is certainly her son is the king of heaven. Marry is the most faithful to God, even before there is no guarantee whom God is but she still obeyed everything, including suffering, even she's without sin. Jesus didn't have the privilege to save us without his death.

Because from the beginning goodness made everything include a God. God is human but because he is so good that is why he is a God. Sinful people like us are not allow to exist. But he knew we wanted to exist so he made our bodies to exist and had to die to save us. So be grateful to our loving God above all love and needs. If God didn't die for us the devil already took us to hell, or we will disappear and become nothing like before. Women are made from men's bone that's why they love them. Imagine God made us out of his whole image how much more he loves us. Before Jesus crucifixion to save us, Abraham rules was when we do sin we will be stoned to death, even only average sins, just to save us from hell, because back then

Jesus did not come down to earth yet to die for our sins so we had to suffered in order to clean our souls. Sex is made out of love. But God is love so he doesn't need sex. That is why Jesus is still single but he is still happy. Some saints like Mary and God have lights appear all around them because they have more love than us, it shines out from their souls. The ancient kings had so many wives, but Solomon said he was still not happy, that is why love feel better than sex. God did make Adam and Eve of other races, but he didn't say everything he did, because it will never end and we can never count. Judas could be forgiven by God if he repented. But he might be Satan in disguise so he hung himself by the other devil forced him to, because he just sold a savior from heaven to die, and other devils came and told Judas must give the money back and go hang himself to be back in hell with them. God is a mercy God, if Judas is that good of a person by repent, God did not let him be the one whom had the most evil sin and be punished the most, so don't worry for Judas. Abortions doctors just wanted to help. But we unintentionally lure them to commit serious crime against God. Embryos are God creations originally, not eggs nor sperms. Eggs or sperms came from Adam and Eve, not made by this couple but by God whom made a body for each of them that had eggs and sperms, but they did not create their own bodies, So abortion is not Adam's and Eve's privilege. Girls and women these days are very lucky that we have pregnancy prevention just by a pill insert into our arms, or other ways. And when we are ready to get pregnant, we just have to get that pill out. This book is from my own opinions about God and everything else. If it's wrong, I hope God will forgive me. And I hope you all don't mind reading it. Thank you. God bless.

Printed in the United States
by Baker & Taylor Publisher Services